ART DECO
DESIGNS & MOTIFS

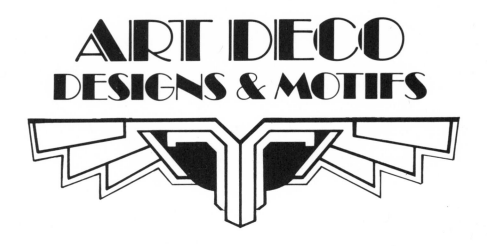

Over 100 Examples Rendered by
MARCIA LOEB

DOVER PUBLICATIONS, INC. NEW YORK

Published in Canada by General Publishing Company, Ltd., 30 Lesmill Road, Don Mills, Toronto, Ontario.
Published in the United Kingdom by Constable and Company, Ltd., 10 Orange Street, London WC 2.

"Art Deco Designs and Motifs" is a new work, first published by Dover Publications, Inc., in 1972.

DOVER *Pictorial Archive* SERIES

International Standard Book Number: 0-486-22826-6
Library of Congress Catalog Card Number: 70-188954

Manufactured in the United States of America
Dover Publications, Inc.
31 East 2nd Street
Mineola, N.Y. 11501

INTRODUCTION

Art Deco is the name now generally applied to the most typical artistic production of the nineteen-twenties and thirties. This name comes from the large exhibition, held in Paris in 1925, called the Exposition Internationale des Arts Décoratifs et Industriels Modernes. The art of these years was extremely varied and eclectic. Its sources included turn-of-the-century art nouveau, most of the important artistic movements that followed (Fauvism, Cubism, Futurism, Expressionism) and such archeological interests of the day as ancient Egyptian and Mayan art.

One of the chief unifying factors of Art Deco is the emphasis on geometrical patterns. Another, related to the first, is the full acceptance of the machine age and the consequent abandonment of the traditional barriers between "fine" and "applied" art. Art Deco has just been "rediscovered" with tremendous impact, and is of major concern to all designers today.

The 75 plates in this book offer over a hundred Art Deco designs based on examples from many branches of the arts, including jewelry, fabrics, stained glass, furniture, metalwork and architecture. The designs have been newly redrawn from photographs of actual objects chosen from numerous authentic portfolios of the period (the portfolios found to be most useful are listed at the end of this introduction). But I have used these sources imaginatively rather than strictly.

Steeped in this period which means so much to me, I have adapted the designs of the in-the-round objects as two-dimensional black-and-white patterns and motifs which can be readily used by graphic designers, package designers, poster artists and advertisers. Of course, this modern reinterpretation of an earlier art period is in the tradition of all applied design.

The designs include many corners, border units and other small motifs that can easily be developed into frames and over-all patterns. I have selected not only a wide variety of geometrical shapes and their combinations, but also some of the animal and plant forms so typical of the era, and an entire large alphabet that is a modern equivalent of the elaborate illuminated letters of the Middle Ages.

In addition, no one interested in coloring can overlook the opportunities Art Deco design provides. Colors can be as wild as you like. Art Deco drew on the "liberated" color of painters like Matisse and the other Fauves, and Picasso. It had a penchant for pastels and reveled in such tints as forest green and plum. No color combinations could be too outré. If you still feel a little timid, look at the sample color treatments on the covers!

Whether you use this book in your work or for pure pleasure, I hope you will share my enthusiasm for this important area of design that has been too long neglected.

M. L.

CHIEF SOURCES OF THE DESIGNS

The series (in many portfolios) "L'Art International d'Aujourd'hui," Editions d'Art Charles Moreau, Paris, c. 1929–1931.

Clouzot, H., "La Ferronnerie Moderne" [Modern Ironwork], Editions d'Art Charles Moreau, Paris, 3 portfolios, n.d.

Martinie, Henri (A.-H.), "Exposition des Arts Décoratifs, Paris, 1925: La Ferronnerie," Editions Albert Lévy, Paris, 2 portfolios, 1926 and 1929.

Virette, Jean, "La Ferronnerie," in the series "Répertoire de l'Architecture Moderne," Editions S. de Bonadona, Paris, 1930.

1

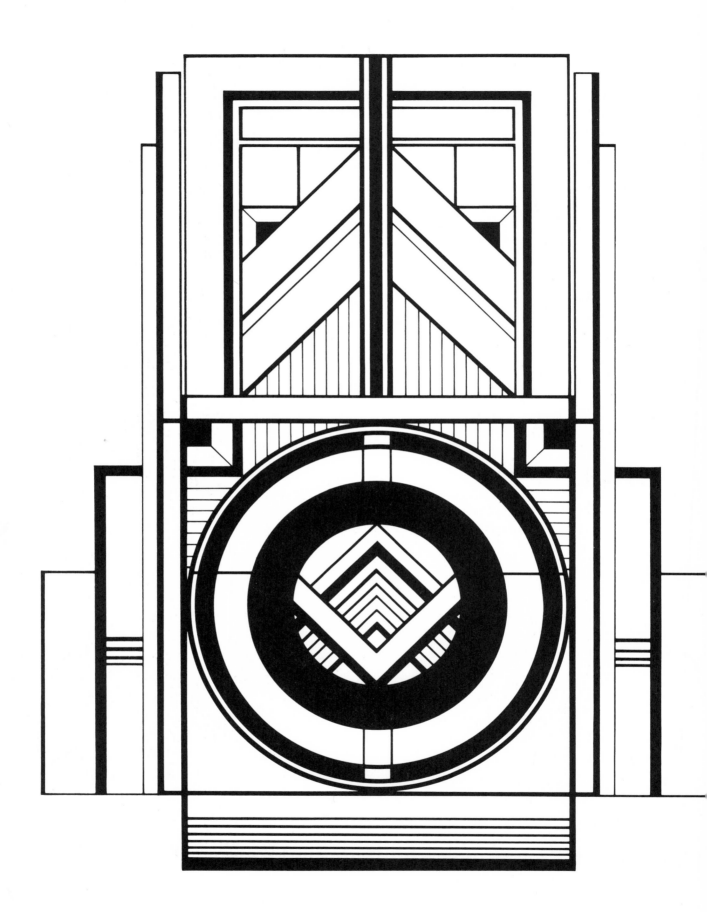

2

4

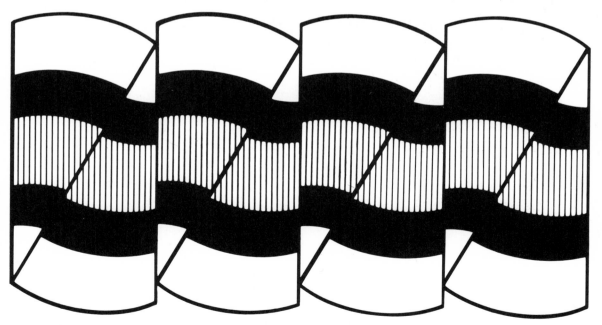

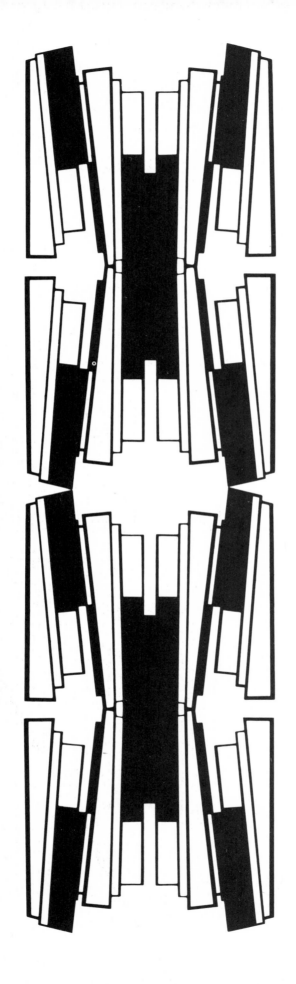

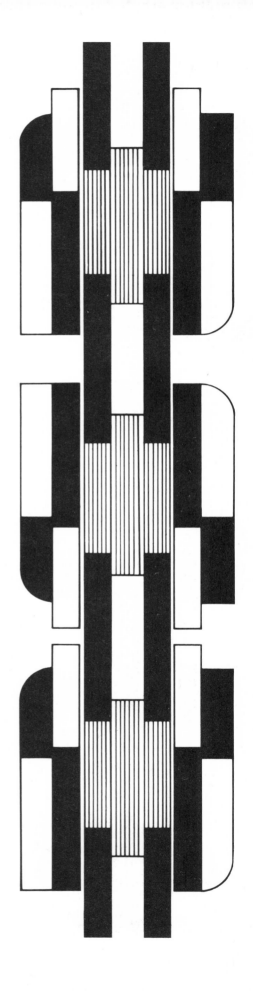

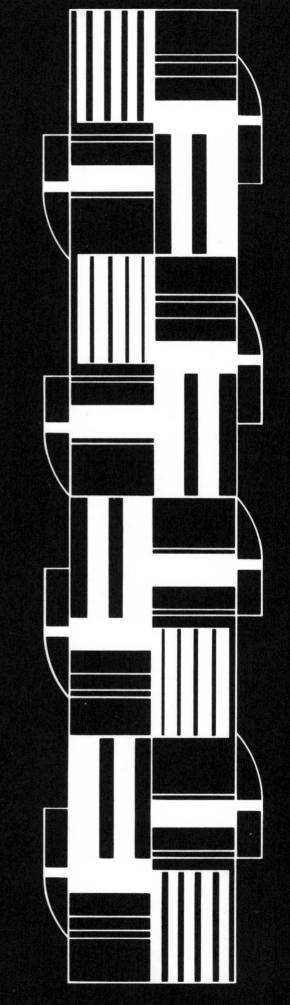

9

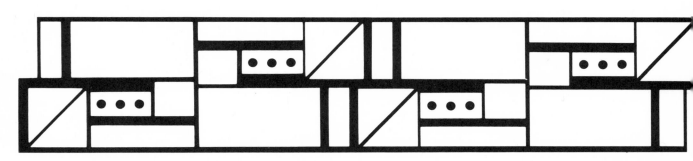

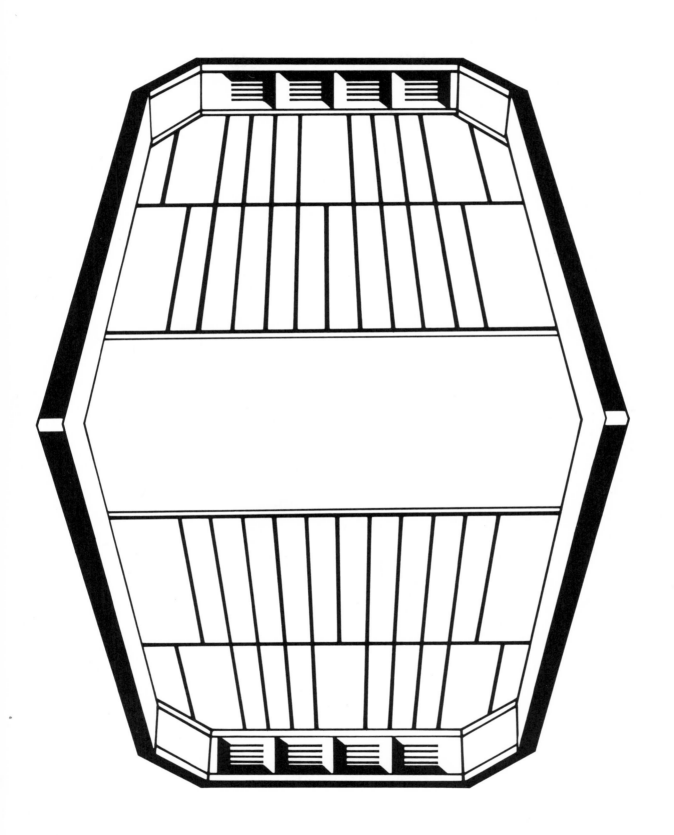

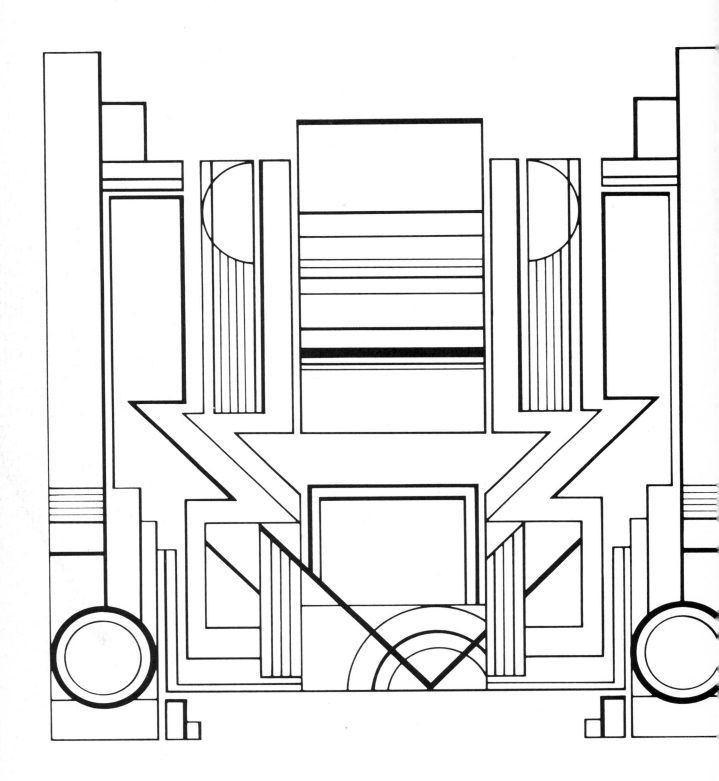

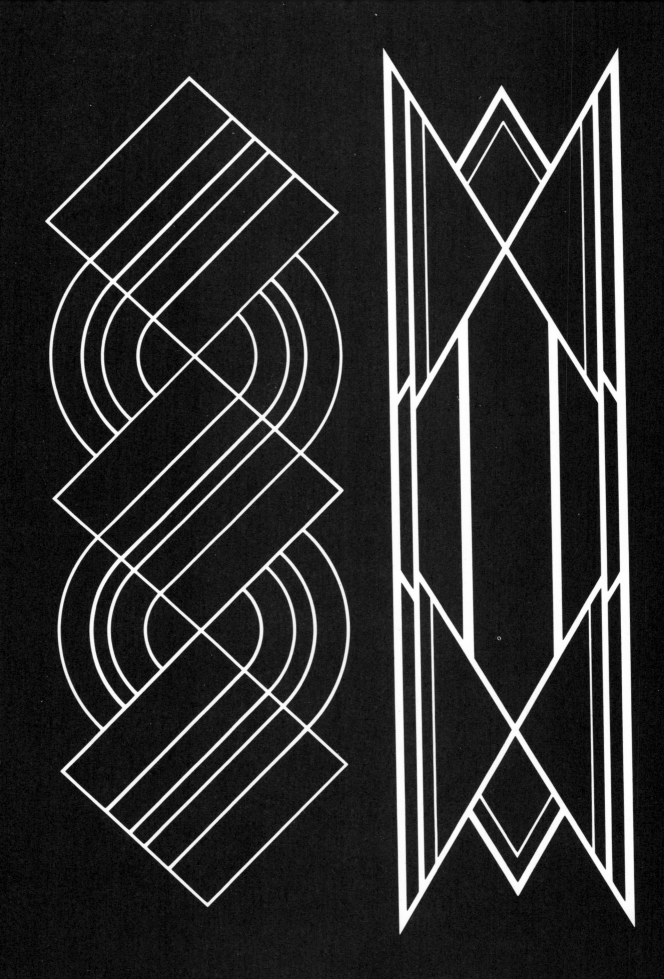

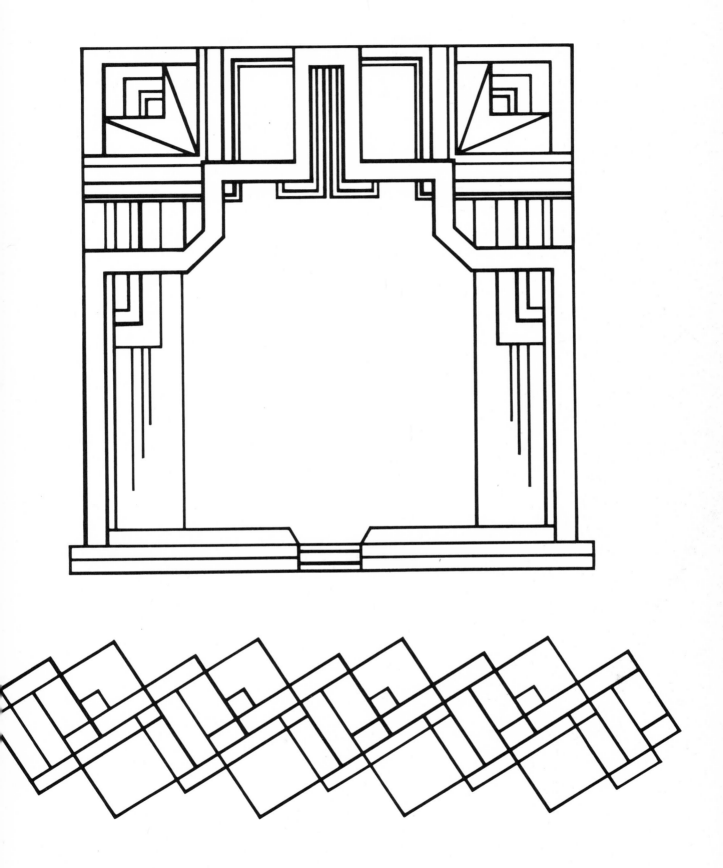

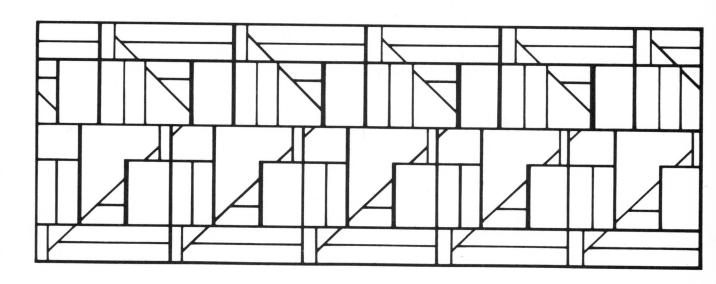

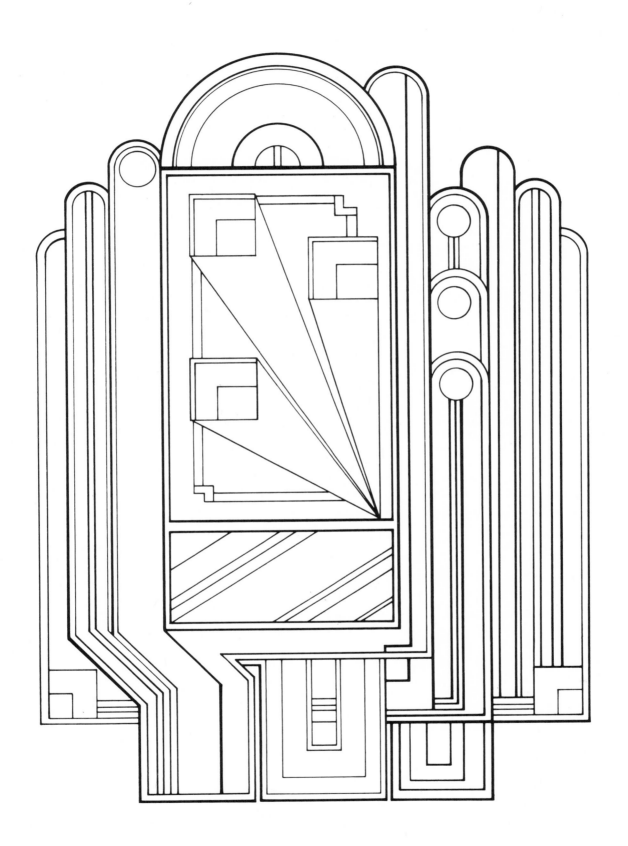

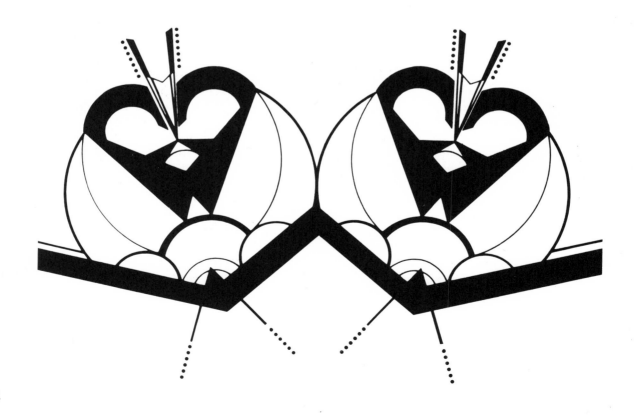

26

30

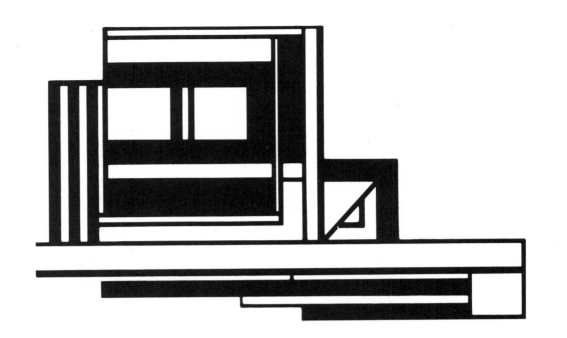

34

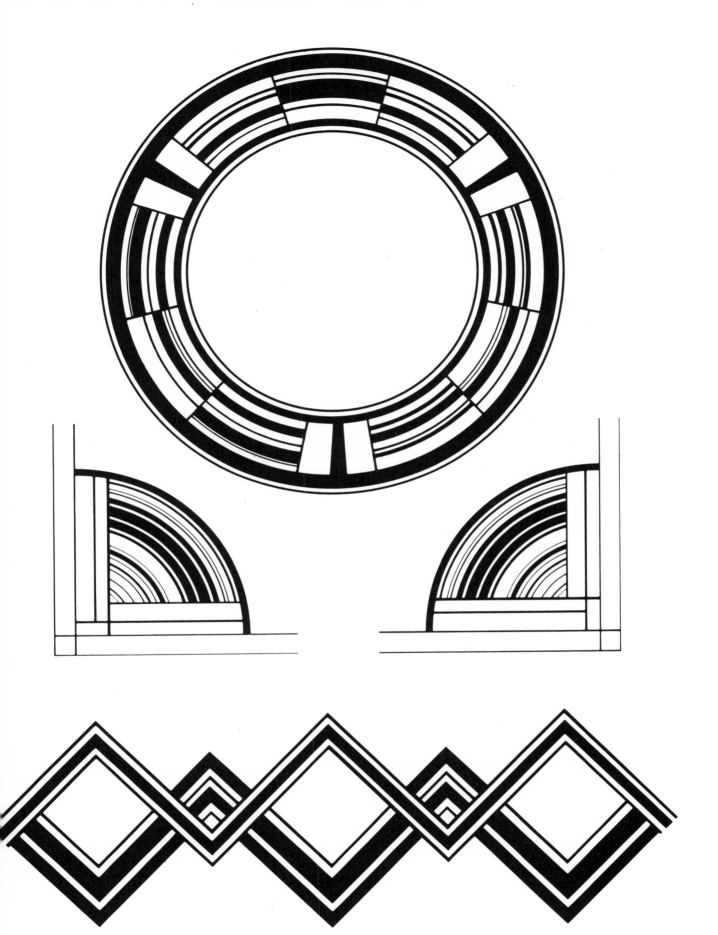

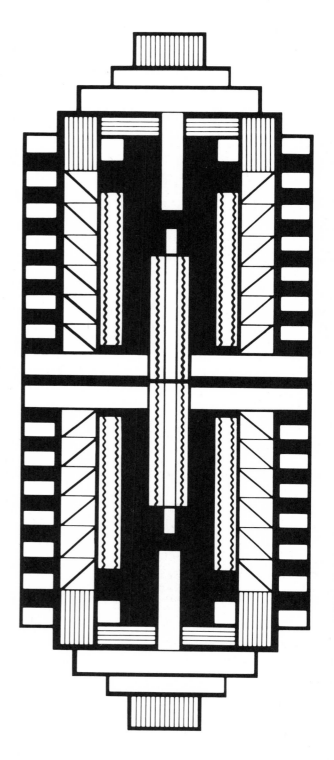

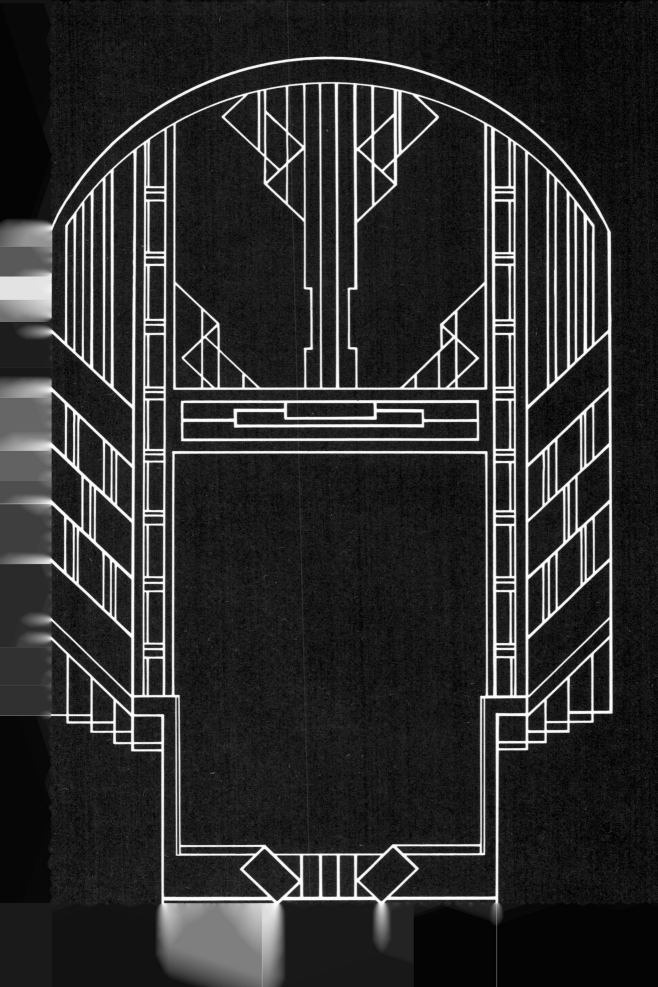

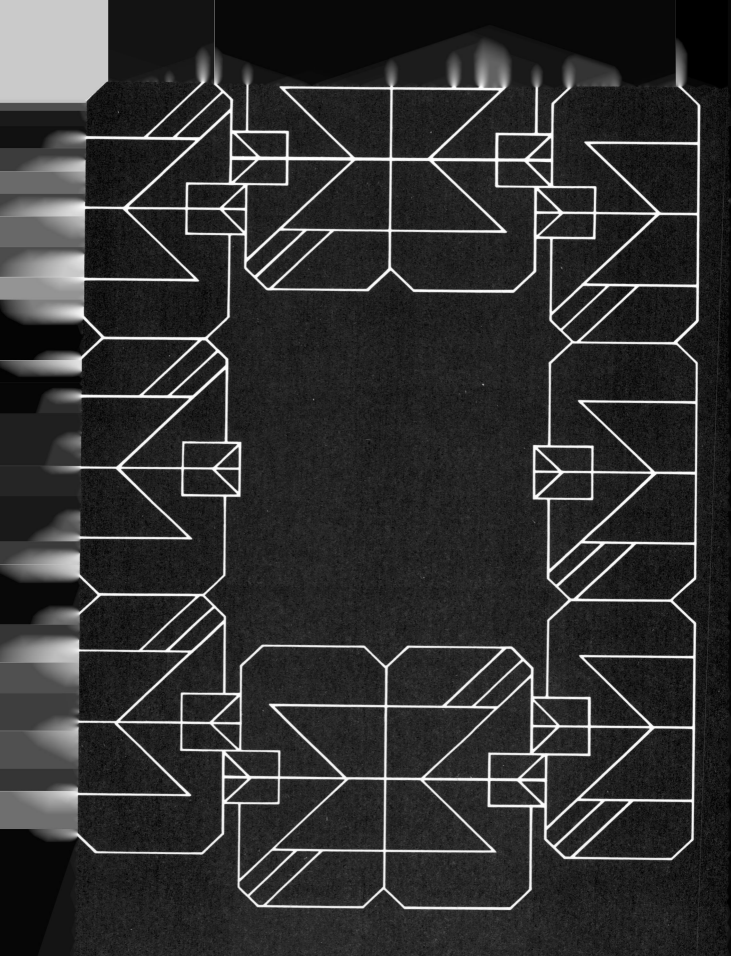

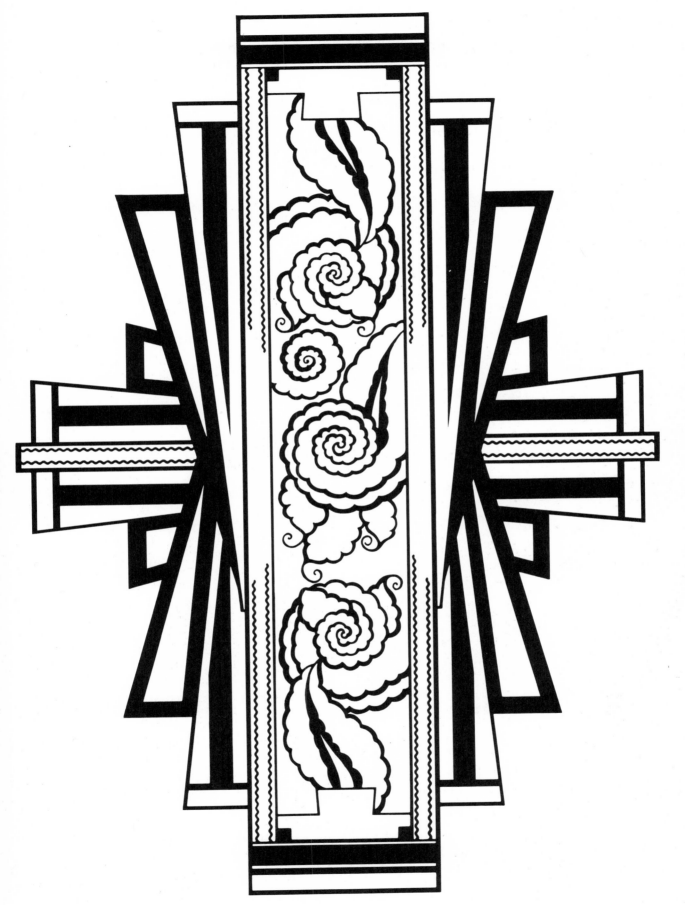

40

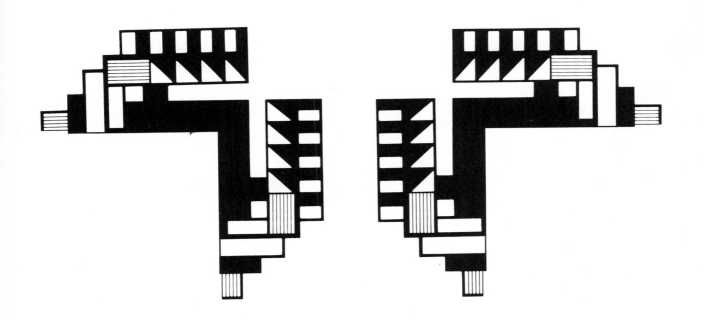

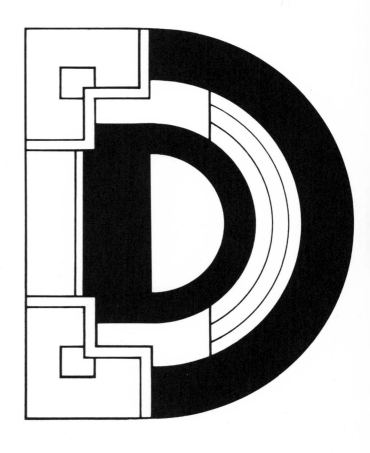

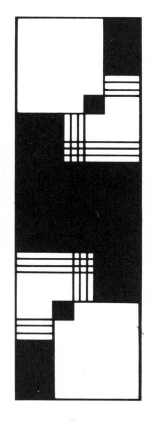

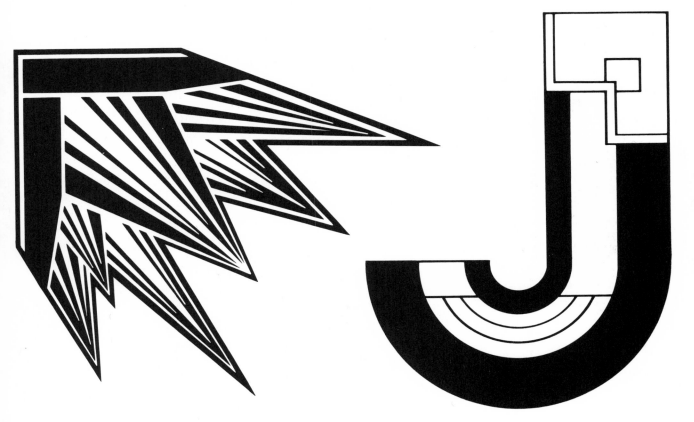

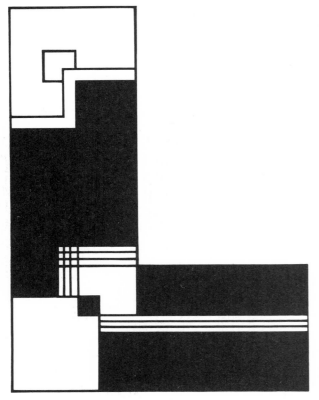

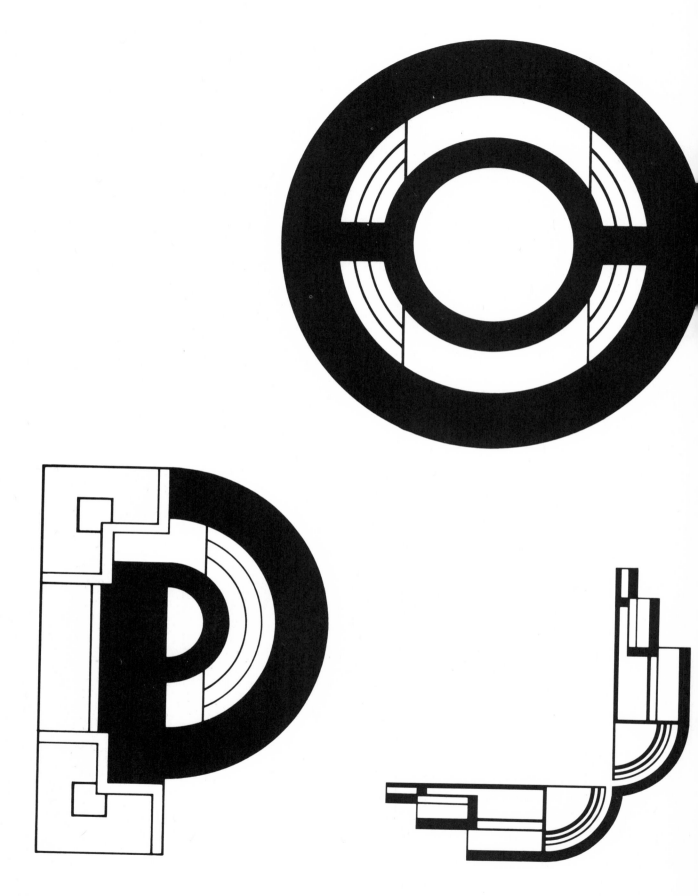

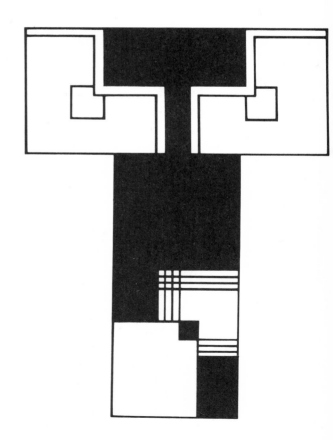

52

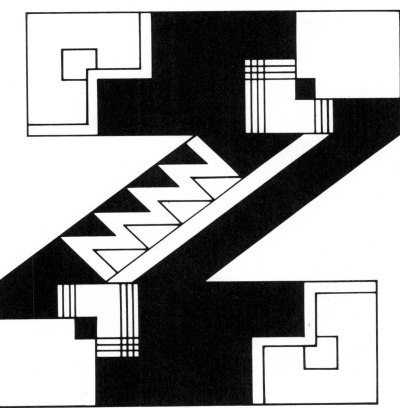

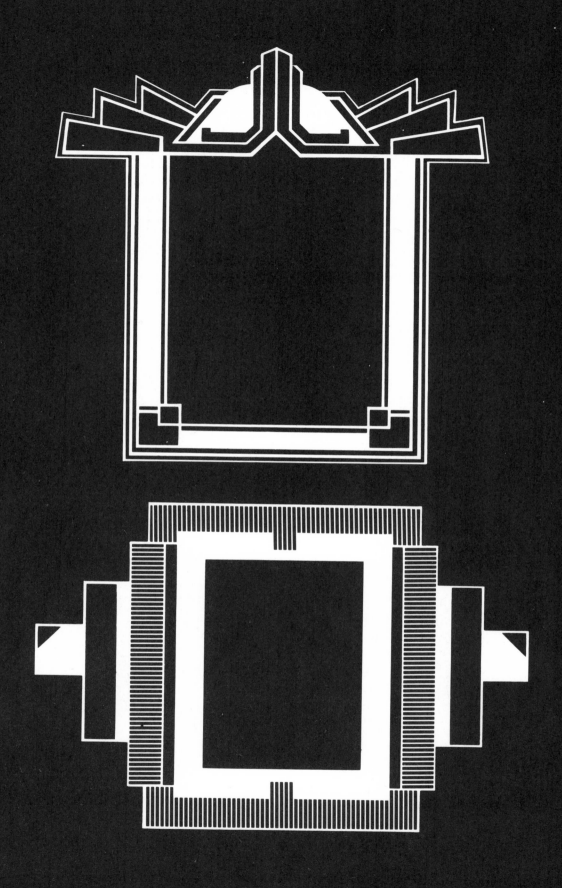

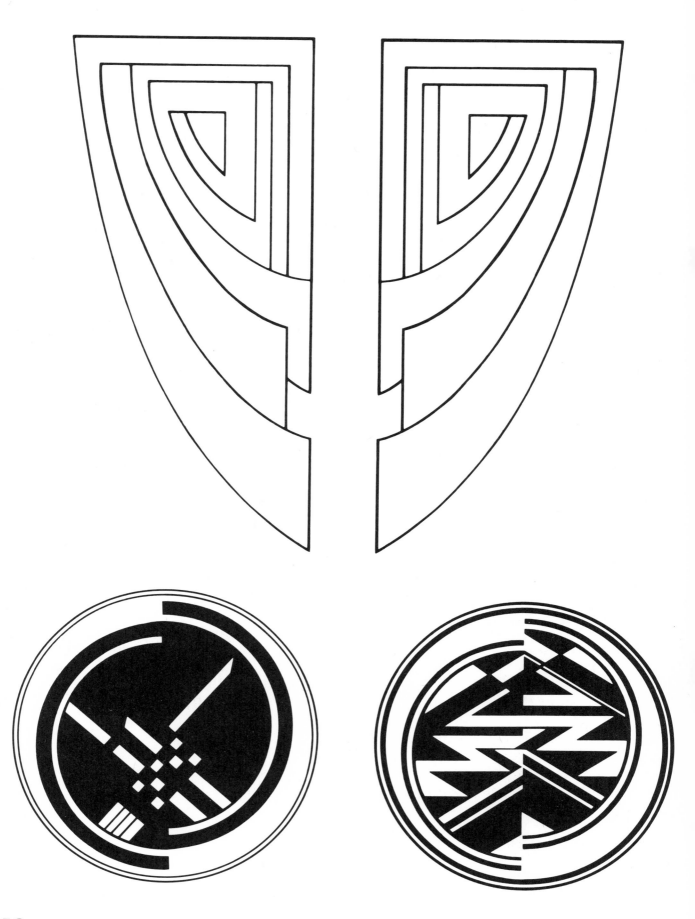

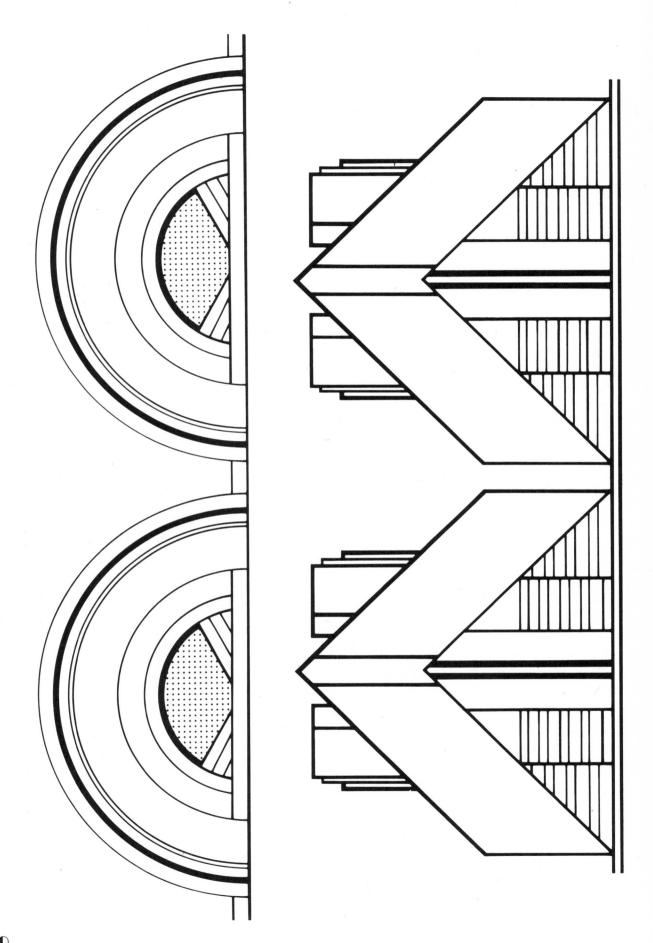

67

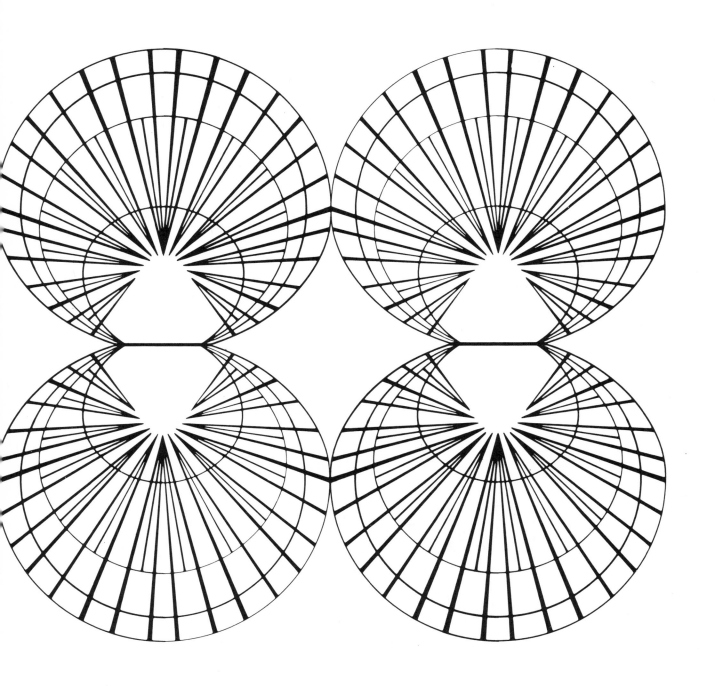

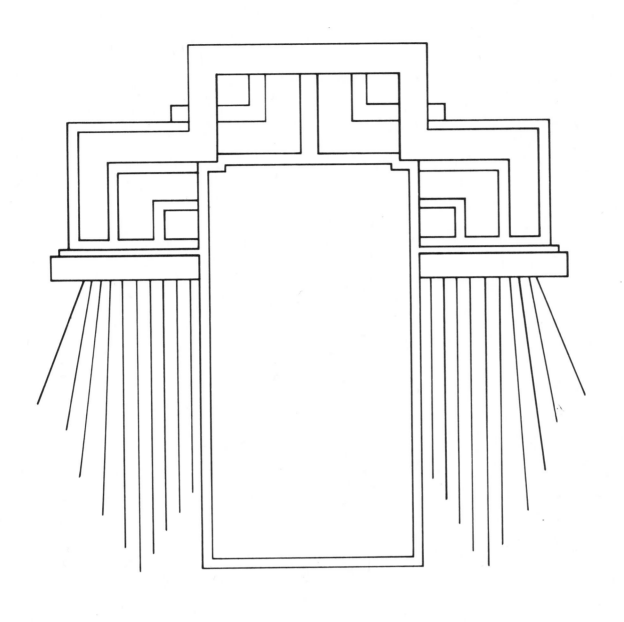

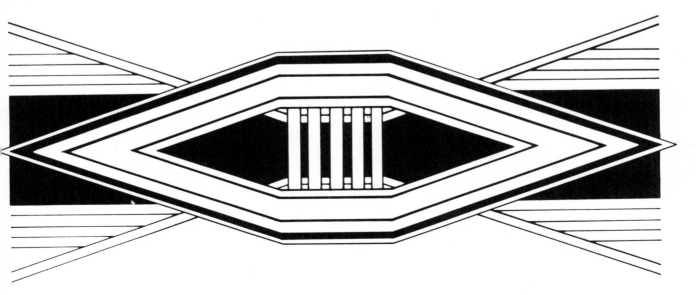

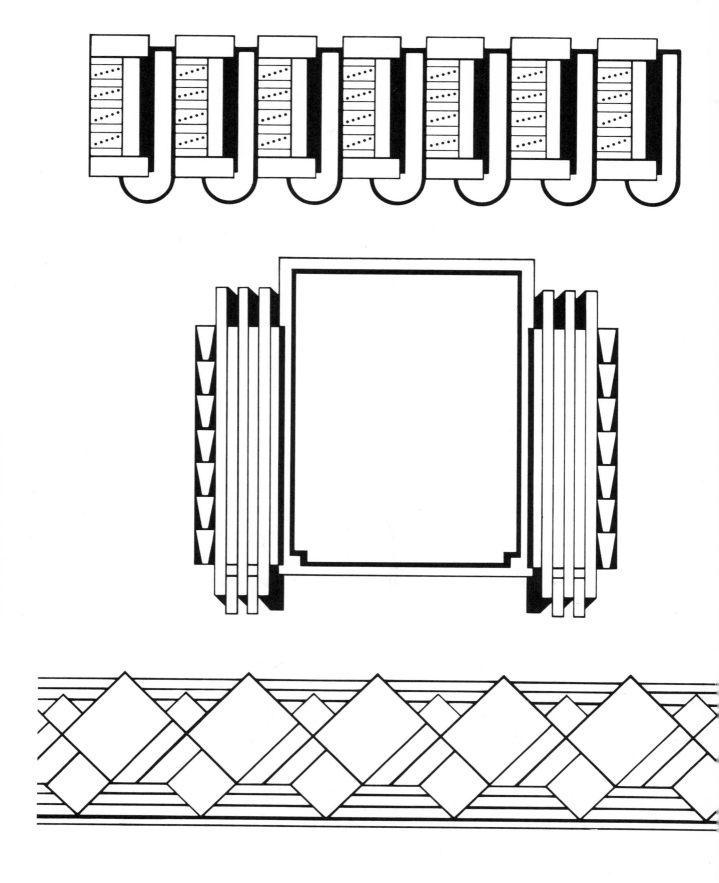